THESE FREAKEN KIDS

The Relationship Between Parents and Their Adult Children

By

Dominic A. D'Abate, Ph.D.

Published by : Consensus Mediation Center
(consensusmediation @me.com)

ISBN – 978-0-9952530-0-1

Cover : Reproduced with permission from a painting by Barbara Sala entitled : Parallel Worlds - Brotherhood
Art wok at the beginning of every chapter courtesy of Barbara Sala

Acknowledgement

The parent - child relationship (including aging parents and their adult children) is considered by many to be the most enduring and long lasting social tie in which human beings engage. This book is dedicated, first and foremost, to all of those parents and adult children who have endured many challenges and setbacks but have rebounded and found constructive solutions and positive alternatives in those difficult times when hope laid in the shadow of despair. Of course, I would be remiss if I didn't express my gratitude to my own parents and siblings who have contributed greatly in shaping my life path.

A much appreciated thanks is equally extended to my many colleagues and friends who have been so instrumental in providing encouragement and constructive feedback with each step I took in finalizing this publication.

Finally, I extend my gratitude to my wife and children who have patiently acted as my trusted sounding board during the many, many months devoted to this endeavour.

TABLE OF CONTENTS

Preface

This book is written, in part, as a response to the growing request from parents who are often dumbfounded and overwhelmed by the conduct and actions of their adult children. How often have we heard distraught parents lament that 'their freaken kids' were driving them crazy, that they act like reckless teenagers who lack any good judgement while refusing to take any advice or threaten to cut off all contact if they are remotely criticized or not given 'unconditional' support. These often desperate sounding laments seem to indicate both a crying need to be heard and an even greater urgency to find ways of coping. The natural and most common response is often to react viscerally in accordance with long held beliefs and parenting practices – "Don't be crazy, listen to what we have to say; You don't know, I've been around the block a few more times than you; here's a budget that makes more sense; I've made another appointment for you, so please keep it this time; you won't be able to support yourself doing that'. In the end, irrespective of the good intentions and 'wisdom' dispensed, parenting an adult child is much like swimming in uncharted waters, while all is calm above, you never know what lurks below or when the next wave is going to come and take you out where you feel least sure of yourself.

Alas, what is one to do or where does one turn? To be certain, in an age of instant information retrieval, the internet is usually the natural place to go as a source of information, having access to a prodigious number of articles, advice sheets and blogs dealing with parent-child relations. Invariably, such a pell-mell of disparate material, including 'how to' recipes and 'suggestions', tend to either obscure matters or reduce complex relational issues and human emotions to quick fix formulas. Adding to the problem is the fact that most people have the tendency to think and analyze issues in a linear, cause and effect manner as it is the easiest way to put things in a logical order and draw conclusions. Unfortunately, this tends to be, for the most part, very unsatisfactory as witnessed by the plethora of forgettable self-help books that have flooded the market in recent years.

Bringing about a change in the way we do things, however, can often be difficult to implement, especially when our thinking is entrenched in traditional approaches that leave little margin for manoeuvre. This publication, aims to present the issues confronting parents and children in a manner that will not only set forth the complex dynamics at play but will also clarify matters enough <u>to</u> <u>enable both parties to envision a new and more effective course of</u> <u>action</u>.

Structure of this Book

This book is structured in a practical and user-friendly format that will highlight typical reactions from parents to common adult children behaviours and provide food for thought in terms of what can potentially be done:

1- **Parental Laments** - Identifying what parents most lament about with regards to their adult children

2- **Natural Reaction** - Identifying the natural reactions of parents based on long held beliefs and parenting practices

3- **Advice and Suggestions** - Outlining what is being said in the literature and suggestions that are being offered by professionals in the field

4- **New Directions** - Adapting to new realities and exploring how things could be different for parents and children.

5- **References** - There is a vast literature (books and articles) and information on the internet that readers can tap for further enlightenment and stimulations.

Unlike most self-help or 'how to books', the content of this publication does not attempt to offer simple answers or ready made solutions to complex issues involving parents and their grown up children. Rather, this book offers information and advice that either party can use in fashioning their own answers and solutions in improving the quality of their unique family relations.

It should be noted that the anecdotes found in this book are taken from reported accounts obtained from individual interviews, response to questionnaires and personal accounts obtained from the internet. Any names used are fictitious in order to protect the identity of those parents who have commented on their experiences. As well, it should be emphasized that parent-adult children relations are not always problematic and that, more often than not, these interactions bring enormous satisfaction and joy to both parties.

Estranged Children - Freaked out Parents

What the Freaken ....

A distraught parent exclaimed in a local newspaper her anguish in having had no contact with one of her adult children since his teenage years even though she always prioritizes his needs over her own and devoted herself to him as a single parent…

…**"The lack of contact with the older one is so hurtful and it makes me so mad, I would like to sever all ties and just forget I have children".**

Another parent projects that it would be extremely hurtful if his child ignored him, especially after the hard work and expense it took to get them to where she is today.

…**"Imagine, after all that I did for her, I don't even get a call, an e-mail or not even a text, a word, for God's sake, it's as if I don't even exist".**

…**"Not having any contact with my child or seeing him was probably the most painful thing I have ever experienced"**

Lamented another distraught parent who had lost contact with her son who simply cut all contact over a disagreement.

…**"I haven't heard from my son in months and I don't even know what I did or did not do to deserve it"**

…**"This is very hurtful and sad, they don't give a damn about our feelings or what's it doing to us"**

…**"That's what you get back after you've given them everything – they're just ungrateful and selfish"**

…**"I love my kids and can't understand how on earth this has happened".**

What on earth is going on …

Estrangement between parents and their adult children is so prevalent that some people consider it to have reached epidemic proportion. For most, being cut off from their children is more than they can bear – what is a parent to do when a son or daughter suddenly decide to cut contact and, in many cases, tells you outright that they never want to have anything to do with you or even the family in which they grew up. When this kind of disconnect takes place, it usually is not short lived but tends to last for an inordinate period of time. Most parents feel victimized and become anxious to normalize relations with their children to what they were before.

While this 'nightmare' can result from the actions of an alienating co-parent as can happen in high conflict separations and divorce, most often it comes as a total surprise and seems to defy any explanation or link to a discernable cause. For the majority of parents, there is a feeling of shame and embarrassment if not humiliation that make it very difficult to either talk about it or attempt to rationally discuss what is truly going on and what events have led to such a calamity. Hence, denial and blame become predictable reactions that, invariably, feed the problem and prevent a focus on solutions, however elusive they may seem. Making matters worse, disagreements and conflict between parents and, especially, co-parents, have a tendency to propel them to 'spin their wheels' and add fuel to an already volatile situation.

The natural response...

Common reactions are often visceral and dictated by how intense the crisis is being experienced. In most instances, parents deal with their pain and consternation by   deferring to their family and cultural roots as well as what is generally considered to be good common sense...

…"There are times when I feel fed up and I just want to cut off all ties with them"

…"I'm so embarrassed and ashamed, I don't want to talk about it with anyone"

…"They'll finally realize their misguided actions and will eventually come around"

…"If you don't pressure them, they're less likely to be antagonistic"

…"Don't let matters be but confront these 'freaken' kids so that they wake up and face the errors of their ways"

…"Become resigned to the fact that things will never improve, after all it's probably our fault anyways – we shouldn't have been so over-protective…"

As these reactions indicate, parents are neither unanimous in their responses nor are they equally resolved to stay the course. For the most part, parents resort to strategies that include accepting their fate and not reacting, hoping for a miracle or taking a hard stance and fighting back. Whatever the reaction, it seems obvious that what worked traditionally in resolving difficulties in family relations, is not nearly as effective when parents are confronted with the actions of their alienating children.

And what do the professionals advise.....

To be sure, much as been written on the subject of the estrangement between parents and their adult children (see reference page at the end of this chapter) and a number of professionals and informed individuals have weighed in with advice and interventions for parents to consider. While some of this advice is based on research conducted by psychologists and other social scientists, other writers and pundits are inspired by traditional thinking and anecdotal accounts of what has proven to be successful.

What parents should know before doing anything

➢ Parents, first and foremost, need to accept some responsibility and vulnerability for what has transpired. Generally speaking, estrangement usually occurs as a process involving both parents and children.

➢ Making an effort to understand your children and how they perceive what has transpired becomes important as a means of opening doors that might otherwise remain closed.

➢ Realize that as children grow up they become less and less dependent on their parents and tend to create distance from them as a means of establishing their independence or even as a protective measure to keep away what they perceive as invasive or abusive parental practices

➤ As families are different, so are children who have their own personality and need to be understood in terms of who they are rather than who they should or might be. Mental health issues and anxiety are often at play and impact their behaviour.

What parents can do

➤ Avoid thinking in terms of whose right and whose wrong as this will only generate blame and a potential escalation of the conflict.

➤ Don't ever give up on making things better while avoiding confrontation and making demands. Often, distancing on the part of children is a *'flight'* response to heightening anxiety that doesn't necessarily imply what most parents feel as *'a hatred'* towards them. Try not to *'cut off'* from them as these children need an opportunity to deal with *'their own'* feelings of rejection.

➤ It is helpful in getting used to expressing oneself in terms of what you feel or desire *('I' perspective)* rather that using the more confrontational approach that starts with *'you'* need to do this or that. Owning one's opinion and feelings and trying to share them with adult children can facilitate an exchange that can lead to understanding and compromise. Get support from friends, family and professionals and avoid going through this painful experience alone.

So, what is a parent to do

For starters...

- Try to understand that what you are feeling as a result of your children's alienating actions while valid and hurtful, are part and parcel of what they, as well, are feeling and experiencing. Actions might not be as intentional or as spiteful as you might, naturally, be lead to believe.
- Give some thought to what relationship issues might have preceded this development. Quite often there is a build up of resentment and ill feeling between your children and you that simply spills over and spins out of control.
- Indicate to your children that you are available and willing to discuss what is bothering them, and this without a time line and urgency.

Avoid...

... acting too quickly on the emotions that these situations generate

... concluding, pre-maturely, that your children 'have it' against you and that what they are doing is, necessarily, deliberate and will persist 'forever'

... having your children's actions create discord with the other parent or co-parent

---

Finding Solutions...

✦ *As parents, you are, after all, human beings who are vulnerable to feelings of hurt and resentment and it is natural for you to conclude that your children's actions are misguided and unreasonable. They may also appear to you as being ungrateful and disrespectful, especially after everything you have done for them.*

✦ *Keep in mind, however, that, despite everything, you are still the 'parents' and expected to react with greater maturity and 'good sense'. Patience, understanding and foresight are in order and it becomes incumbent on you, unless otherwise indicated, to keep the door of communication open until an honest discussion between you and your adult children can be had.*

✦ *Dealing with these stressful situations can take time and a toll on you. Be open to sharing your frustrations and grief with the other parent and even professionals when necessary.*

Check these references...

Publications on Parent – Adult Children Relations and Estrangement:

✓ "Study of relationships between adult children and parents." Medical News Today. Retrieved from Swanbrow, D. (2009, May 6). http://www.medicalnewstoday.com/releases/149047.php.

✓ « Estrangement Between Mothers and Adult Children: The Role of Norms and Values ». Megan Gilligan J. Jill Suitor Karl Pillemer . Journal of Marriage and Family (2015). web.ics.purdue.edu/.../publications/Estrangement.

✓ Hidden voices - Stand Alone – Dr. Lucy Blake. University of Cambridgestandalone.org.uk/wp-content/uploads/2015/12/HiddenVoices.FinalReport.pdf

✓ When Parents Hurt: Compassionate Strategies When You and Your Grown Child Don't Get Along. Dr.Joshua Coleman. (HarperCollins). Visit him at http://www.drjoshuacoleman.com/

On the Internet:

- Estranged Stories - Understanding. Support. Peace. Hope http://estrangedstories.ning.com

- Parent with an estranged adult child support group:

    http://www.dailystrength.org/g.....iscussions

- Empowering Parents

    www.empoweringparents.com

- Parents of Estranged adult Children

    www.dovechristiancounseling.com/Parents-of-Estranged-   Adult-Children.html

- Rejected parents of estranged adult children - Welcome www.rejectedparents.net/
- Family provision - are parents obliged to provide for an estranged www.bartier.com.au/publications/publicationDetail.aspx?PublicationIThe
- Epidemiology of Estrangement http://tinagilbertson.com/estrangement-guide-1/

Aggressive and Critical Children – Indignant Parents

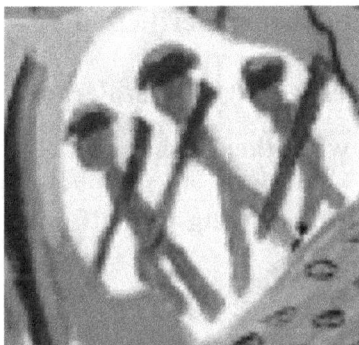

What the Freaken ....

All too often parents decry the critical and disrespectful behaviour on the part of their adult children. Most are shocked and in disbelief at what they hear and are made to endure. A disheartened mother was devastated by how she was treated by her children…

… **"I can't believe it, my kids think I'm a complete idiot".**

Another parent was disillusioned and perplexed

…**"While they were growing up, we were made to think that we knew everything and could fix anything - suddenly, the message is that we really don't know 'squat' and what we have to say is irrelevant and of little use to them".**

Some other parents related how their children's behaviour had such a demoralizing and painful effect on them…

…**"Being told that we are old, senile and not in tune with the 'real world' is hurtful and demeaning".**

…**"I don't deserve this abusive behaviour – I can't say or do anything any more without being put down and criticized".**

…**"My children have become so disrespectful and intolerant, I hardly recognize who they are and what they've become".**

…**"I can't tell my son anything for fear of being told off and made to feel like some old babbling fool".**

A number of parents expressed resentment and even anger towards their children…

…**"I don't deserve this treatment – I'm still their parent, you know".**

…**"This is extortion – I was told to pay up or else! Imagine, this is my child who grew up in a loving home and he threatens me!!"**

What on earth is going on …

Children can become unusually critical and often aggressive in their relationships with parents who, invariably, feel shocked, confused and indignant by the manner in which they are treated. In some instances, the reproach takes the form of mild reprimands (you eat badly, are inactive and don't have a social life) while, at other times it takes the form of a more condescending, judgemental and critical remarks (you're stingy, getting senile and becoming more controlling and nosy) that focus on perceived personal defects and faulty behaviour. For the most part, parents are made to feel deficient in their thinking and actions while left wondering as to whether all that is being said is actually merited or unwarranted accusations. Irrespective of how it is being interpreted, most parents feel diminished and at a loss as to how they should respond.

Of greater concern is when such reproaches take on a more malicious overtone and border on abusive treatment of parents by their seemingly insensitive and unabashedly critical adult children. Increasingly, some parents become unwitting victims of abusive or venomous language, accentuating blame, censure or even bitter, deep-seated ill will. Threats of dire consequences (physical injury or abandonment) are not that uncommon when parents refuse requests for money or don't agree to give them what they feel is their rightful inheritance. There are also numerous accounts where parents have been strong-armed to sign over family property only to be left in cold without a place to stay. For many parents, this abusive behavior appears to come out of nowhere and does not seem to be justified by anything past or present that these parent victims have done. In fact, some experts consider this trend to be a rapidly growing social problem plaguing elderly parents.

The natural response...

Shock, disbelief and profound disappointment are typical reactions on the part of parents when confronted by aggressive and manipulative children. Even admitting to the fact that their children are inappropriate or abusive in the manner in which they are treated becomes a very stressful and difficult thing to do. In response, some will defend themselves by confronting their critical and antagonistic children while most will resign themselves with a 'grin and bear it' attitude for fear of further escalating the conflict. This resignation can all too easily turn to despair due to, among other things, the lack of control over what happens in their lives.

One parent exclaimed her confusion over her daughter's 'sudden' aggressive and unexplainable critical attitude towards her.....

... "I'm not sure how to deal with her pushy attitude and these demands....maybe all of this will pass and things will get back to what they were".

Another parent became so anxious over his children's critical remarks and insistence that he change his own behaviour that he became quite demoralized and started to second guess himself....

..."You know, maybe they are right, I'm really not sure of anything anymore, I don't want to make things worse, they have enough to worry about"

When being subjected to violent or abusive behaviour, it is not unusual for victimized parents to become fearful of being harmed or abandoned if they retaliate or refuse to comply

... "God, I don't know what to do, who do I turn to.. whose going to believe an old man"

... "Go to the police, complain... sure and then what?"

Unfortunately, for many the isolation, feelings of vulnerability and lack of confidence in themselves make it easier to have the attitude of

..."Better to accept the devil you know than the one you don't".

And what do the professionals advise...

Generally speaking, tensions and disagreements between parents and their adult children (from discontent to conflict) are considered normal and can result from a variety of developmental causes usually related to the parent-child relationship across the lifespan of the family. On the other hand, aggressive and abusive behaviours are much more serious actions that can often be pernicious and put parents at risk.

What parents should know before doing anything

➢ For starters, parents need to assess the actions of their adult children and determine if there is any justification or reasonable cause. There is the possibility that a parent's own actions (talking too much, over intrusive behaviour, nagging, etc.) may be provoking their criticism, comments or verbal attacks. Understanding one's own contribution to the conflict and self disclosure to the adult child of how you feel and what you expect can greatly facilitate the search for solutions and what each party can do to normalize relations.

➢ Parents need to rely on their wisdom and resourcefulness as they have previously done in their lives to help them navigate these rough waters. Despondence and resignation is a parent's worst enemy and should be replaced with positive and hopeful thinking that a better family narrative will emerge.

➢ It's possible that the behaviour of adult children is affected by their own personal disposition or what they are experiencing in their life situation (stress, mental health issue, financial problems). While this does not make it right, you may be but a convenient and familiar target for letting out their frustrations.

Actions parents can take

➢ As with other issues that parents are forced to deal with, it is imperative that help is sought from family, friends and professionals who can shed more objective light on what is happening.

➢ Convincing your adult children to seek help and support even if you have to pay for the intervention of a professional.

➢ Parents need to create a united front, particularly with spouses (or co-parents) and other children and family members that are willing and able to help find solutions.

➢ Parents have a right to ask their adult children to treat them with respect and dignity and to put an end to verbal, physical or financial abuse. If all efforts fail to ward off the unwanted behaviour, parents need to engage the legal system to force their children to stop before more serious consequences and damage are inflicted.

➢ When anger becomes a driving force, it is probably wiser to step back and not engage immediately in a conflict that can easily escalate and spiral out of control.

So, what is a parent to do…

<u>For starters</u>…

- You need to tell yourself that aggressive and abusive behaviour is not part of a healthy parent-adult child relationship and that there are probably underlying causes to this toxic interaction

- Step back when being confronted and try to be mindful of what exactly is being said to you or to the other parent. Ask yourself if this is actually related to present circumstances or has to do with past events or old disputes.

- Ask yourself if anything you are doing is fuelling the aggressive behaviour

---

<u>Avoid</u>…

… becoming overly discouraged and despondent when confronted with behaviour that is aggressive or abusive

… lashing out in anger and becoming enmeshed in an escalating conflict that can only make matters worse

---

Finding Solutions.....

- Aggressive and abusive behaviour towards you on the part of your adult children can incite you to retaliate or become a passive victim – in either case, the result is anything but satisfactory and, worse, can spiral out of control. Doing something different becomes essential in stemming and putting a stop to the negative interaction (e.g. getting your adult children to express their needs).

- As we have concluded in the previous chapter, solutions are not easily attained and require a great deal of patience, perseverance and, quite often, for parents to set limits as to what is acceptable behaviour towards them. When boundaries are set, you and your adult children can more successfully engage in a process of uncovering more positive and desirable ways of relating. Getting support from other family members and professionals can facilitate this process.

Check these references...

<u>Publications on Aggressive and Abusive Relations:</u>

✓ **Handbook of Dynamics in Parent-Child Relations.** edited by Leon Kuczynski. Sage Publication, 2003. Books.google.com.

✓ **Schiamberg, L. B., & Gans, D. (1999). An ecological framework for contextual risk factors in elder abuse by adult children. Journal of Elder Abuse & Neglect, 11(1), 79-103.**

✓ **Passive-Aggressive Example: Disrespectful Attitude from Adult Child** https://www.excelatlife.com/pa_examples/12.htm

✓ **Understanding Oppositional Children - ASCD** www.ascd.org/publications/books/.../Understanding_Oppositional_Children.aspx

✓ **The Cost of Blaming Parents | Greater Good** greatergood.berkeley.edu/article/item/the_cost_of_blaming_parents

<u>On the Internet:</u>

- **How Adult Children Manipulate Parents | Empowering Parents** www.empoweringparents.com › Ages & Stages › Adult Children

- **How to Handle Your Overly Critical Adult Kids - Bottom Line** Inc.bottomlineinc.com/how-to-handle-your-overly-critical-adult-kids/

- **When a Mother says She is the Victim of her Adult Children** emergingfrombroken.com/when-a-mother-says-she-is-the-victim-of-her-adult-children/

- **How to Deal With Rude Adult Children** www.livestrong.com › Parenting

Out of Control Finances – Overwhelmed Parents

What the Freaken ....

Compared to the previous dilemmas faced by parents, financial issues are often considered to be less critical and important, that is, until they face serious consequences.

Dismayed parents lament in disbelief how children could have duped them and left them out to dry…

…**"I signed over my home to my kids hoping that I would live there in peace until I would die. Instead, I now find myself living alone elsewhere and barely able to provide for my daily needs".**

…**"I gave to the point of becoming needy myself. When I asked my children for help, their response was 'we can't'. I ended up in a nursing home with inferior care".**

Some parents are put in such a double bind that they clearly are uncertain as to where to turn…

…**"We are stuck between a rock and a hard places, because we want our children to be happy".**

Other parents question the very situation in which they find themselves…

…**"We don't mind helping you, but do we really need to subsidize your 'lattes', kale salads, pedicures and countless of other expenses you can't seem to do without".**

…**"When we were young, we did without or at least stayed within our means – we certainly couldn't get our parents to bail us out".**

What on earth is going on?

A Financial Post headline (September 2, 2015) read: *Parents financial supporting adult children feeling the pinch provides an interesting exposé to what is considered to be a nearly epidemic phenomenon.* A recent CIBC survey concluded that over two thirds of Canadian parents reported feeling a real burden when supporting adult children and lamented how this is putting a real damper on their ability to save for their retirement. Financial support of adult children includes subsidizing education, rent, food, cell phones, cars, entertainment and even vacations. Aside from the very affluent, most parents are, consequently, obliged to do with less and deprive themselves of the anticipated benefits of their 'golden years'. Worse, they are often forced to take money out of retirement saving plans and not paying down mortgages. In the U.S. the situation is much the same. Some research findings on the subject further conclude that when either parents or children worry about finances, other problems or issues in the family tend to be exacerbated. A July, 2014 survey by American Consumer Credit Counselling found that one in three households provide assistance to their adult millennials.

The natural response...

It is quite normal for parents to want to help their adult children but when does it become a financial burden and creates overdependence? Some children, for example, buy homes they can't afford and leave their parents stuck with paying the mortgage to avoid default. Nevertheless, despite the often-dire consequences, parents, like superman, will most often come to the rescue and impulsively act against their better judgement or past experiences.

..."In time they'll eventually learn to spend less than they earn"

...**"You can't take it with you anyways, so better that you make it available now that they need it"**

...**"If financial help stops, they'll end up in the street, on drugs or dependent on others that won't have their best interest"**

...**"They'll hate me for not supporting them and I'll loose all contact with them"**

...**"Just as well to give it to them now when they need it most and not after I die"**

...**"We should make life easier for our children as opposed to the hard times we experienced"**

...**"Nothing should be spared for their higher education, it's the best investment we can make for our children"**

And what do the professionals advise...

Questions over financial issues involving 'baby boomers' as well as some older 'generation X' and their adult children have been a favourite musing found in countless articles and even books written on the subject. The following represents the gamut of so called 'good advice' to distressed parents who seek some solace or direction in their efforts to help their children.

What parents should know before doing anything

➢ By helping too much, parents will run the risk of jeopardizing their own financial situation and contributing to fostering entitlement and dependence that prevents their children from assuming responsibility and control over their future. Bailing out these children doesn't necessarily do them any favours in the long run.

➢ It's a bad idea to fund their adult children without any accountability as they need to learn that they have to stand on their own two feet and develop better ways to cope with their financial predicament.

What parents can do

➢ Have your adult children assume responsibility for their post secondary education (loans, bursaries, part time jobs) as this will make them feel more invested in their career paths and not bankrupt you in the process.

➢ You ultimately want your children to be able to deal with 'their' financial realities when you are no longer there to help them.

➢ If you are inclined to give them large sums of money to help with major investments (purchase of homes or investment in a business) make the money available as a loan.

This is especially prudent given the many unforeseeable events (divorce settlements, bankruptcies) that might all too often arise and undermine your generous offering.

➢ When your children convince you in investing in a 'fantastic business opportunity' protect yourself legally so that you can, at least, recoup some of your money and not be liable for debts incurred.

➢ If you are inclined to support your children's graduate studies make sure that they have a realistic and well thought out plan with a reasonable time frame.

➢ Encourage and motivate your children to be resourceful and find ways in which they can rely on their own resourcefulness and abilities to make it on their own – a free lunch can often have the opposite effect.

So, what is a parent to do...

For starters......

- Sit down and make an inventory of what you have (assets, income) and, importantly, what are your projected needs as well as those family members that are still dependent on you.

- Doing this basic accounting exercise will give you a heads up on what you can afford to do in helping your children (how much, when and how).

Avoid...

... *being impulsive* in reacting to any financial demands made on you

... *a sense of obligation* or guilt in compelling your decision to help

---

Finding Solutions...

+ Most parents are generally *hard wired to assist their children* in whatever way they can and will often do so automatically without giving much thought as to the consequences for themselves and *those they help. While this is a natural tendency, parents would do well to base their decisions <u>on a more rational process</u>.*

+ *Asking yourself <u>what it is</u> <u>that would change or be different</u> for you and your adult children if you were to help out financially can allow you to more effectively weigh the pros and cons that such a decision might have sometime in the future.*

+ *Involving the other parent and the children (and perhaps even a financial advisor) in the process will ensure that whatever financial help is provided will be most beneficial and constructive for your adult children and, at the same time, minimize any potential negative impact on you.*

Check these references...

<u>Publications on Adult Children and Finances:</u>

✓ Financial Transfers from Parents to Adult Children - Population ...
> www.psc.isr.umich.edu/pubs/pdf/rr01-485.pdf

✓ Growing Parental Economic Power in Parent-Adult Child Households ...
> https://www.researchgate.net/publication/235691048
> > Growing_Parental_Economic_Po..

✓ Children and Money: Teaching Children Money Habits for Life
> www.extension.umn.edu/.../personal-finance/.../adult.../teaching-children-money-   habi...by T Dunrud

✓ Grandparents raising their grandchildren: A review of the literature and suggestions for practice
> B Hayslip, PL Kaminski - the Gerontologist, 2005 -
> gerontologist.oxfordjournals.org

✓ Between elderly parents and adult children: a new look at the intergenerational care provided by the 'sandwich generation' . <u>E Grundy</u>, JC Henretta - Ageing and Society, 2006 - Cambridge Univ Press

<u>On the Internet:</u>

- Later life parents helping adult children - Australian Institute of Family ...
> https://aifs.gov.au/publications/family-relationships-and.../later-life-parents-helping-

- How Parents Support Their Adult Children | Family Studies-family-studies.org/how-parents-support-their-adult-children

- How to Avoid Paying for Your Kids Forever - Time
  time.com/money/page/parents-adult-children-financial-
  support/

- Strategy for supporting your adult children | Ameriprise
  Financial
  https://www.ameriprise.com/.../financial.../personal-
  finance/strategies-for-supporting-a...

- When To Cut The Financial Cord On Your Kids |
  Bankrate.com
  www.bankrate.com/finance/personal-finance/cut-financial-
  cord-on-kids-1.aspx

In and Out of the Family Home - Parents in a Frenzy

What the Freaken ....

Parents have mixed reactions when dealing with adult children who are reluctant and even refuse to leave the family home or un-expectantly show up at their door. For some, this situation is not normal while others are caught in a dilemma of not being certain in terms of how to react. One thing is certain, whether their adult children stay or come back, parents experience a frenzy of emotions…

…**"Both my children have become way too comfortable staying at home, they are never going to leave".**

… **"My heart skipped a beat when I saw my son coming up the driveway with two suitcases in hand…I hadn't heard from him in almost a year".**

…**"I think something is wrong with this picture- I go to work everyday and my 28 year old daughter stays home and watches soaps and walks the dog".**

…"She's moving back home with her kids, how do we deal with this catastrophe?"

Some parents feel they are between a rock and a hard place…

…"If I ask him to leave, I'll never see him again"

…"What do you want me to do, she's old enough to be on her own but she's diagnosed with ADD and gets depressed so easily. How can I ask her to go on her own".

And the unbearable stress and family tensions generated by a sudden return home…

…"Since he's come back, he stirs up so much trouble with his younger siblings…this can't continue"

What on earth is going on?

Adult children who won't leave the comfort of their family home or come back to the parental nest due to unfortunate and unanticipated circumstances not only put parents in untenable binds but push the boundaries of what is a reasonable and acceptable parental response. Those hard laid plans to finally enjoy the 'golden years' without worry and parental responsibilities become elusive and not so easily attainable. According to reliable sources, a majority of parents are forced to continue providing for their so called 'independent' children and even grandchildren who, at times, have no other support on which to fall back. In the U.S., census figures estimate that nearly 53% of 18 to 24 year olds and nearly 25% of those aged between 18-34 still live with their parents. This represents well over 25 million young adults. Of those attending college and university, nearly 80 per cent or approximately 2 million return home and remain there indefinitely. In a recent Wall Street Journal article, it was reported that 60% of 10,000 grandparents surveyed provide some sort of financial support to their adult children and grandchildren. The average cost to parents per adult child per year can vary between $8,000 to $20,000 depending on what frills parents throw in i.e. entertainment, travel, pocket money, car. While some parents can absorb these extra costs, albeit not easily, others have to assume extra debt (re-mortgage the family home or take out a loan) and are hard pressed to retire at a reasonable age.

Reasons for leaving home may include more desired independence, conflicts with (or between) parents, going off to college or setting up a household with a significant other. Not leaving in the first place can, conversely, be motivated by insecurity and fear of the outside world, not finding the 'right job', unwillingness to give up a pampered existence and not finding anyone else with whom they could live. So why has this, now, become such a common phenomenon and one that is increasing at an alarming rate. The answer lies partly in the fact that financial hardships caused by a downturn in the economy and the job market (especially in European countries) force adult children to seek support and security in a familiar and more hospitable setting. Reduced capabilities due to mental illness, drug dependence and relationship breakdown will also push them to stay or return. Added to this, is fact that 'baby boomers' are easily thrown into a frenzy of guilt, a sense of personal failure as a parent and confusion as to the 'right way' of dealing with this less than normal situation.

The natural response ...

Some parents find it very hard to set their children adrift and let them struggle on their own while others are of the belief that young adults should leave the proverbial nest sooner rather than later and are not expected to return. However, there appears to be a prevalent sense of parental obligation and sympathy that permeates most thinking and decision-making. If their adult children are indeed being lazy or opportunistic, many parents would hardly know it ....

...**"Okay, you can come back home, we'll figure it out"**

...**"My son has lost his job, it's not his fault in these hard times...how can I throw him in the street"**

..."They are in the waiting room but they wouldn't know when the train has arrived for them"

Not unusual are the parents who dread being left alone in an empty nest...

..."I can't imagine living alone in this huge house"

In some cultural communities, marriage is the appropriate time to leave the family home, especially for young women. In most instances, moving out can be within a stone's throw ...

..."I pray that my youngest daughter will follow the lead of her sisters and finally settle down "

..."Now that they are married, they can live upstairs...why rent to strangers"

And the ultimate rationalization for a grandmother...

..."If they're here, I can watch their children while they go to work"

And what do the professionals advise.....

In general, parents face a dilemma in that they want to be supportive of their adult children while ensuring that they move forward towards independence and self-sufficiency. Great frustration is usually felt when these adult children want to be treated as adults but are unwilling to pull their weight and assume their responsibilities in the household. Who is in charge and who has the final say are questions that confront parents on a daily basis.

With few exceptions, 'empty nesters' who are unexpectedly obliged to deal with returning children, often referred to as the 'boomerang kids', also face particular challenges in their efforts to cope. It is acknowledged that the impact is greater on parents when children come back unexpectedly as they then have to consider a change in plans (retirement, travel, downsizing) with no 'exit plan' on the horizon. Consequently, there is an increase in stress and a lowering of satisfaction with the way things have turned out. Unfortunately these distressed parents are at greater risk of becoming abused and subject to some sort of mental health problem or diagnosis such as dementia, depression and even Alzheimer.

Many parents also feel sandwiched between the responsibility of caring for aging parents who are dependent on them and having to continue or resume the care of adult children in the home. The strain is as much on the nerves as it is on the pocket book as parents have to, once again, re-negotiate family tasks and roles and share precious time and energy.

What parents should know before doing anything

➢ Getting adult children out of the family home and into the world can strain parent-child relations. At the same time, it can be viewed as an act of love that can, in the long term, help them to become independent and self-sufficient. Continuing to shelter them, on the other hand, will only encourage inaction and feelings of insecurity.

➢ Adult children tend not to leave the family home because their lives have become too comfortable and there is no incentive to leave. Allowing the status quo to continue makes it difficult to move forward and bring about change.

➢ Sooner or later, it becomes essential that adult children who are not in school should be out in the work force. To be sure, that first job might not be ideal but it is a start. Developing a good work ethic and paying expenses is a necessary first step moving forward towards responsible adulthood.

➢ When young adults return home, they have, usually, fallen on hard times financially or in their personal and social lives or have just finished school and have little direction. They need some temporary respite and refuge at best but not necessarily permanent residence.

Structured parenting with rules and clear expectations

Being stuck with adult children in the home can be turned into an excellent opportunity for 'maturing children' to learn how to tend to their needs by having to do chores around the house, take care of their clothing, shopping, cleaning and assume responsibilities for their finances. If they have been living in a dorm or on their own, it's not unusual for them to want to continue with what they have become accustomed. Parents need to redefine the parameters and rules of living at home.

➤ Parents should listen and keep the lines of communication open. At the same time, they should also be ready to provide guidance and clear boundaries that they can enforce.

➤ Major conflicts can be avoided if all parties are clear about their roles and expectations in the home e.g. cooking, cleaning, covering expenses, use of car.

➤ When adult children remain in the home, they are usually in need of some respite, motivation and insight as to what to do and where to go. Parents can be very helpful if they convey to their adult children that they absolutely need to assume responsibility for dealing with their predicament and that they will provide for their needs in a reasonable manner.

Confusion when adult children are also parents

It's one thing to have your adult son or daughter show up at your doorstep with their bags in hand, but it's quite another when they show up with their own children tagging alone. Obviously, while most parents will welcome them with open arms and heart, the situation remains problematic in that new roles need to be created to fit the situation. Being grandparents at arms distance is not the same as having your grandchildren live with you and poses different challenges.

➢ Clarifying the parenting roles and tasks from the beginning can go a long way in preventing confusion later on as to who has the ultimate authority as well as the responsibility for the care of grandchildren.

➢ When parents are faced with poor parenting skills, every effort should be made to help these new parents 'build capacity' as opposed to simply taking over their parenting roles and responsibilities.

➢ When adult children are absent (incarceration, live-in detox program) and not able to fulfill their obligations towards their own children, parents sometimes need to step in and fill the vacuum. Hopefully, this will only be temporary and the terrain should be prepared for their eventual return and resumption of their roles.

Having an adult child leave the home

Sometimes, parents are confronted with untenable situations whereby an adult child still living at home or having returned creates such tension and conflict that they are asked to leave.

➤ When the presence of an adult child in the home is disruptive or even detrimental to the well being of the others, a parent needs to take the necessary steps to remedy the situation. It is wise to check one's motives and not do anything based solely on heightened emotions (anger or fear) but on safety issues. Parents need to be clear as to what they need to communicate to a wayward son or daughter and demand that specific changes be made.

➤ Insist that the conditions are not negotiable and that if they cannot be followed, then leaving the home becomes necessary. Mean what you say and avoid making threats that cannot be carried out. Seeking the advice of a professional can be useful when you are really stuck.

➤ And then there comes a time when a parent has to say to their off-springs that "it's time to move on as this arrangement is no longer working for you''. Such a statement should be made firmly and in a manner that conveys love and concern for their best interest.

So, what is a parent to do...

For starters ...

- Have a discussion at the parental level so that both of you, as parents, are on the same page and can present a common position and limits that can be conveyed to your adult children in any future discussions.

- Bring the family together and begin a discussion with regards to everyone's plans and expectations as well as the rules and time frame that will apply to remaining or returning to the family home.

<u>Avoid ...</u>

... being unclear as to what you want or expect your adult children to do

... making decisions unilaterally without their input

... assuming responsibility for their situation and finding solutions for them

---

Finding Solutions.....

- *Parents of adult children who need to leave the family home or return for a variety of reasons are faced with many challenges that require much thoughtful consideration and tough decisions that, often, need to be made. A parent needs to exercise good judgement while also being understanding, compassionate and fair.*

- *On the whole, whatever is decided should not be done unilaterally but, necessarily, needs to include all parties involved.*

- *As adults, children need to be treated as being capable of, ultimately, taking responsibility for their own care and survival and empowered to move forward with their lives. Parents can be most helpful when they help their children generate viable options for themselves and assume responsibility for what they do or don't do.*

Check these references...

Publications on Adult Children In and Out of the Family Home

✓ Does your family push adult children to leave the nest?

scholar.princeton.edu/gkaplan/files/move_back_home_cb c_canada.pdf

✓ The Boomerang Generation | Pew Research Center
www.pewsocialtrends.org/2012/03/15/the-boomerang-generation/

✓ An empty nest can promote freedom, improved relationships
www.apa.org › Monitor on Psychology › April 2003 Monitor on Psychology

✓ Young adults living with parents in the UK - [ARCHIVED CONTENT ...
www.ons.gov.uk/ons/rel/family-demography/young-adults.../sty-young-adults.html

On the Internet:

- Adult children living at home - Legal Aid NSW
www.legalaid.nsw.gov.au › Publications › Factsheets and resources

- Family Matters - Issue 36 - Young adults living at home | Australian ...https://aifs.gov.au/publications/family-matters/issue-36/youngadults-living-home

- Older Adults Challenged Financially When Adult
  Children Move Home
  healthpolicy.ucla.edu/publications/Documents/PDF/.../Ad
  ultChildrenPB-feb2014.pdf

- Family Matters - Issue 36 - Young adults living at home |
  Australian ...
  https://aifs.gov.au/publications/family-matters/issue-
  36/young-adults-living-home

- Stay Close to Your Kids When They Grow Up - Bottom
  Line Inc.
  bottomlineinc.com/how-to-stay-close-to-your-kids-when-
  they-grow-up-and-move-aw..

- Leaving home: Independence, togetherness and income
  in Europe
  www.un.org/en/development/desa/.../publications/.../2011-
  10_Iacovou_Expert-paper....

Reaction to an Unexpected Parental Separation and Divorce – Confused and Embarrassed Parents

What the Freaken ....

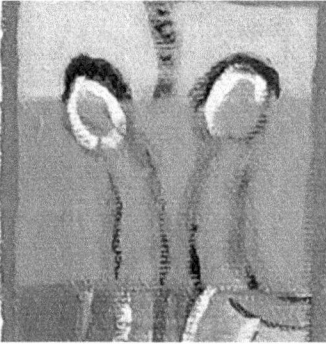

While parents hardly plan to separate or divorce their long time partners, when it occurs, it can leave one or both in a tailspin and wondering just what happened and how to tell their children. Feelings of guilt, anger and most of all, shame, further complicate their future relations with their adult children and their families. To be expected, their reactions don't make things any easier but rather tend to stir up already heated emotions.

In most situations, parents are confronted with very tough questioning (for some bordering on an inquisition) and being expected to explain what seemed obvious to them…

… "Why am I forced to justify why we decided to divorce and what's the reason for it…she asked if we were fighting or if one of us was having an affair"

Other parents are shocked at the fact that their children don't understand that the divorce was in everyone's best interest and needed to happen…

… "You'd think they would be happy for me, I needed to do this to move on to a better place… instead I'm being treated as insensitive and self serving…no compassion at all"

Still others can't believe the lack of maturity in their children's reaction to their decisions to divorce…

…"You would swear I had announced the end of the world… I would have expected a more reasonable and more grown-up reaction from my so called adult children"

… "Why are you so upset, you're grown up"

… " I've been accused of undermining my daughter's life and ruining her long term relationship…she never even told me she had serious plans with someone"

Not uncommon, is the guilt trip parents are made to feel for their actions…

… "My son emphasized that what we did ruined his life and that he now questions everything about his own life and beliefs…this really upset and hurt me as there was always such a strong bond between us"

What on earth is going on?

While it has become common knowledge and the subject of a burgeoning literature that the rate of separation and divorce over the past 25 years has increased for the general population, the number of 'gray' divorces has also been on the rise. According to information obtained from various sources in both Canada and the U.S., while this rate is starting to stabilize for most married couples, there is an alarming increase in the divorce rate attributed to the 'baby boomer' generation, especially those over 50 years of age. Researchers have found that the number has doubled since 1990 and that one in four divorces were attributed to this population. Even among octogenarians who have spent over 50 years together in a supposedly happy union, the number of separations and divorces are inordinately high. Interestingly, this phenomenon cuts across socio-economic status, religious affiliation and even cultural background. In fact, it's not even a strictly North American occurrence as this increase has been observed in many other countries.

The reasons given for ending a marriage are many but those considered to be triggers have to do with the 'empty nest syndrome', finding a 'younger partner', the extra time couples spend together as a result of 'early retirement' and the fact that most baby boomers live longer and anticipate many years still

47

ahead of them. Irrespective of the root cause, the impact is huge and profoundly significant in changing the family landscape and, more importantly, in how parents and their adult children perceive and relate with each other. Traditional values and religious convictions are often put to the test and uprooted while parents, for the most part, are made to feel the brunt of their decisions which are seen as being ill conceives, impulsive and inconsiderate. To this litany of blame, parents, instinctively, end up engaged in some sort of damage control and trying to make sense of it all from their own viewpoint.

The natural response.....

So, what's the big deal! Well, perhaps this population of divorcing parents appears to misjudge and even deny the real possibility that the impact that these break-ups have on family life and on adult children, in particular, is far greater than they could imagine. Mistakenly, there is a conviction among many of these parents that adult children are less likely to be traumatized by their actions because of their age. Such misperceptions, unfortunately, create the illusion that 'all is well' and a 'business as usual' attitude. When they are faced with the fall-out and negative reaction from their children (and other family members) it is more than they can handle and, consequently, various lenses are used to view and rationalize what has and is happening.

A common belief is that these children can eventually handle the announcement and the new reality. After all, they are adults now and should be more mature in how they react…

…"I know they are hurt and confused by all of this…everyone is, believe me…but they are not little children and I know that eventually they'll come around and understand"

…"I have only my children to talk to about this horrible thing that happened…there's no one else I can turn to"

…"My children should know everything so that I don't get blamed for the family falling apart"

Some parents convince themselves that their children will be able to straighten out their marital problems…

…. "If anyone can talk to some sense to him it's my son, he's the only one he'll listen to"

And what do the professionals advise…..

In most instances, parents can be oblivious to the fact that their separation or divorce is an earth shattering event, a blockbuster that can easily topple many previously held beliefs and traditions of family life. It can easily undermine the level of security, self-confidence and reliance on values and a way of life, usually on the part of adult children, that were once considered by them to have been stable and inviolable. To be sure, adult children also underestimate their need to consider how they complicate matters and what they also need to do while parents can equally underestimate the need to step back and take another sober look at how family life has changed.

There is certainly no lack of opinion or advice on the part of those who consider themselves experts in these matters as to what parents should or should not do. The following provides a synopsis of what professionals feel are important considerations and steps to take to improve relations between parents and their adult children prior to or following a decision to separate or divorce:

Announcing the separation or divorce

➢ While it seems an obvious and logical thing to do, parents have a difficult time announcing to their adult children that they plan to separate. There are different ways to do this with dignity and respect, but essentially it boils down to: announcing the decision together to all your children; avoid attributing blame or responsibility; try to keep strong emotions under control; spare your children the unpleasant details; put the focus on what will necessarily change and how the decision will impact on the children; expect an emotional reaction and, finally, try to weather the storm as it most likely will create plenty of turbulence.

Children caught in a conflict of loyalty

➢ Much like younger children, adult children can also be put in a conflict of loyalty whereby they are obliged to choose from the 'good parent' and the one who is 'bad' and responsible for the whole mess. Sometimes parents facilitate this process by recruiting allies among their children and trying to convince them that they are right and the other parent is the culprit.

➢ It's important to avoid fighting or engaging in any denigrating and blaming behaviour that puts the other parent in a bad light, especially in front of the adult children.

➢ Problems related to intimacy and infidelity have to do with the parents and not with the children.

Assuming responsibility for needs of the other parent

➢ Depending on the extent to which one of the parents was dependent on the other for various tasks or needs (financial, medical, physical or emotional support) the adult children can be left with the, often, onerous responsibility of filling in for the missing parent. If separation or a divorce are unavoidable, it would be desirable if arrangements were made in advance to ensure that the needs of *the parent in question would be provided.*

Questions over finances and family assets

➤ Invariably, questions over money, financial obligations and family assets and inheritance tend to surface as major concerns and points of contention when parents decide to split up. It would be helpful if parents were more aware of the impact these issues would have on each other and their children and take the necessary steps to ensure better planning.

New significant others joining the 'family'

➤ If a new partner enters the picture, their impact on family relations and functioning can be significant. While always a delicate and difficult issue, the parent in question should be sensitive to their children's reactions and judicious in how these new partners are integrated into the family. Financial issues also come into play and should be addressed by the parent with some input from the children.

Getting help and support

➤ Family break-up at whatever age and irrespective of who initiates it and who feels victimized by it is one of the most difficult life events with which to cope and adjust. All parties concerned are usually obliged to deal with a myriad of conflicting emotions, financial and legal issues and having to face family, friends and other significant individuals (employers, religious elders). It's wise and, in some cases, necessary to seek help and support from formal or informal sources and, in the process, avoid putting undue pressure and undue stress on your adult children.

Parental modelling and family narrative

➤ What you do as parents will invariably be scrutinized by your children and, to one degree or another, integrated into their own repertoire – you're a role model even at their age. As well, parenting and family life continues and so does the family narrative of which every member is a part. Parents should help their children and grandchildren relate to a positive family story and leave them with a legacy of which they can be proud.

So, what is a parent to do...

For starters.....

- However difficult it may be, both parents need to announce, preferably together, their impending separation or divorce to their adult children. It is important that the latter hear the same explanation (without blame and culpability) from each of their parents.

- Settle all financial matters between you and your spouse and decide together how to include the children in the partition of the family patrimony

- In a timely manner, introduce all new partners who plan to be part of your life to your children

---

Try to avoid...

... individually announcing to your children that you are getting separated or divorcing

... avoid giving the details, especially which parent is responsible and for what reasons

... taking on the role of the helpless victim as your children will be obliged to come to your rescue, something they might ill afford to do

---

Finding Solutions.....

+ Dealing with one's own entangled emotions in time of a separation or divorce is hard enough, but the reaction of adult children can be even more unnerving and anxiety producing. As with younger children, the reaction can be overwhelming and create serious and long lasting disturbance in family relations. In other words, there is no easy way to calm the waters other than keeping any emerging conflict from escalating.

+ As everyone is probably invested in preserving a positive family narrative, it is important that family traditions and practices be maintained as much as is possible under the circumstances.

+ Taking care of yourself is primordial, as it will allow your adult children to worry less about you and focus on their own family life.

Check these references…

Publications on Adult Children of Divorce:

✓ Parental divorce and adult well-being: A meta-analysis
  <u>PR Amato</u>, <u>B Keith</u> - Journal of Marriage and the Family, 1991
  – JSTOR

✓ The long-term effects of parental divorce on the mental
  health of young adults: A developmental perspective   PL
  Chase-Lansdale, <u>AJ Cherlin</u>… - Child …, 1995 - Wiley
  Online Library

✓ The effect of parental divorce and remarriage on parental
  support for adult   children   L White - Journal of Family
  Issues, 1992 - jfi.sagepub.com

✓ Later life parental divorce and widowhood: Impact on young
  adults' assessment of parent-child relations   WS Aquilino -
  Journal of Marriage and the Family, 1994 - JSTOR

On the Internet:

- 8 Things Adult Children Of Divorce Desperately Want You To
  Know …
  www.divorceandchildren.com/tips-for-parents-of-adult-
  children-of-divorce/

- What Nobody Tells You About Being an Adult Child of
  Divorce - Mic
  mic.com/articles/…/what-nobody-tells-you-about-being-an-
  adult-child-of-divorce

-   From a grown up child of divorce - practical guides and a
  place to rant …
  thegrownupchild.ca/

- How to Move on From Your Parents' 'Grey Divorce' - Huffington Post
  www.huffingtonpost.com/.../how-to-move-on-from-your-grey-divorce_b_5242932.h..

- Adult children carry the burden of divorce too - The Globe and Mail
  www.theglobeandmail.com › Life

- Stop Telling Adult Children Of Divorce To 'Get Over It' - Role Reboot
  www.rolereboot.org/.../2013-12-stop-telling-adult-children-of-divorce-to-get-over-

Adult Children in Crisis – Distraught Parents

What the Freaken ....

As parents aren't always aware when their adult children are in the midst of a life crisis, their initial reaction, once they are made aware of it, is usually one of disbelief, shock and denial…

… **"This cannot be happening to my son...I would never have imagined he would ever put himself in a situation like this!"**

… **"There must be some mistake – Jesse would never do such a thing"**

… **"In our family?…what the hell is going on.."**

Panic stricken and distraught, parents seldom take the news well…

… **"This is the worst news…I'm so heart broken?"**

… **"My poor grandkids, they don't deserve this"**

… **"After three failed jobs, my daughter is rudderless and getting depressed"**

The initial shock can easily turn to anger and frustration…

… **"What on earth was he thinking of…no consideration for any of us"**

… **"If only she would have listened to me and taken my advice, we wouldn't be in this bloody mess"**

What on earth is going on?

The common belief is that parents work hard in bringing up their children and after all the years of sacrifice in getting them to adulthood, they can finally put their stress aside and enjoy the fruit of their hard labour. For all to many disillusioned parents, however, the congratulations are premature and the deserved respite not forthcoming. What all too often await them are unexpected events that can, literally shake their world. Their children's promising career path, the seemingly stable social life and newly formed family circles can come tumbling down. Their emergent adult years as well as in latter periods of their life cycle can bring risk and trouble in the form of substance abuse (alcohol, drugs), serious physical and mental health problems, family break-up, incarceration and even suicidal attempts on the part of their adult children. Compounding matters for parents is the fact that they are seldom aware that something is wrong until these potential life-altering situations become full-blown crisis.

The natural response...

It is safe to say that parents are not at their best when finding out that their adult children are experiencing a major life-altering crisis. In fact, as can be seen by the following typical reactions, their response is often not fully thought out or based on an effective problem solving strategy. In fact, it is not unusual to have parents who 'check up' or even 'spy' on their children once they become aware that they are struggling. Even if one of several children is in distress, such an occurrence can impact adversely a parent's own mental health and well-being. Commonly, parents have a tendency to either abdicate any responsibility and further intervention or to become over involved in solving their children's predicament. Aging parents, are, particularly, negatively impacted by crisis in the family and are most apt to feel despondence.

Frustration, anger and feelings of disempowerment can push parents to detach and put distance between themselves and their children's problems...

... "I just don't care anymore, this is more than I can handle!"

... "She doesn't listen, just like her mother... so now what do you want me to do...it's a little late, you know"

... **"I'd like to help but, right now, I'm retired, I can hardly deal with my own problems"**

Some parents are inclined to do the opposite and end up being overly involved in a rescue mission that often puts them over their heads...

... **"Just when I'm ready to pull out, they draw me in..."**

... **"You know, a parent's job is never finished, ever...their lucky they have us around... "**

... **"I can fix this mess but their mother needs to get on board and not fight me "**

... **" We really have no choice but to sell the house..."**

It doesn't help when one parent undermines the other ...

.... **"I was finished paying for courses he kept failing but his father gave in and paid for new programs at another place"**

And what do the professionals advise.....

When children are young, parents normally step in, take charge and find solutions to presenting problems but when they are dealing with older children, the situation becomes more convoluted and complicated. Assuming parental responsibilities and obligations in time of crisis is easier said than done and turns what might seem like solvable problems into potential nightmares and disasters. Some adult children who find themselves in critical situations are unwitting victims of circumstances beyond their control. For others, bad decisions and misguided lifestyle choices create untenable situations from which they can't easily extricate themselves.

Parents dealing with hard-pressed adult children are invariably faced with the dilemma of coming to their rescue while, at the same time, wanting to encourage their competence and independence. For many, the easier course of action, obviously, is to simply be pro active and not wait for the crisis to get out of hand. It is a lot harder to just sit back and be available, listening and allowing the adult children to try and find their own solutions. Therapists working with adult children frequently complain that well-meaning parents all too often interfere and intrude on a process that belongs to their off-springs and not to them. What a parent may think is the right thing to do or the right way to think might not necessarily be what their children need or is acceptable to them.

What parents should know before doing anything

➢ Your adult children are, perhaps, much more able to eventually deal with their own crisis (or what might appear to be such). Before rushing in to help, do some fact finding as to the degree and extent of the problem and how well (or not) your adult children cope.

➢ Providing unsolicited advice or direct help may open up a Pandora's box of old issues and feelings that were never dealt with and that still remain explosive. Caution is strongly recommended.

➢ It is quite easy for parents to become overwhelmed (financially, emotionally, physically) and divided in their actions. Support each other and get support for yourselves as well as for your children.

Differentiating when and what assistance is helpful

➢ Parental assistance can take the form of financial help or simply providing emotional support and guidance to direct action. It's crucial for parents to assess when their children should weather their misfortunes themselves and when direct help is essential. Also important is for parents to stand united and establish firm boundaries.

➢ It is wise for parents to stand by their principles and sometimes use 'tough love' to guide their intervention. While this can be a difficult decision to take when a loved one's well being is at risk, being a 'helicopter parent' prevents them from developing self reliance and resourcefulness.

➢ Intervention for a problem that doesn't put anyone in danger is probably more warranted if the problem directly involves the parents themselves or the grandchildren who tend to be very vulnerable.

Parental engagement when assistance is required

➢ Parents should refrain from intervening or providing solutions before their adult children indicate that there is a problem and that they need help.

➢ Parents need to acknowledge the adult status of their children and convey to them that, irrespective of what help is provided, they are ultimately responsible for the mess in which they find themselves and the solutions that need to be implemented.

➢ When therapy is the recommended course of action, parents need to be mindful of the fact that it is not up to them to direct the process. Adult children need to go through their own painful process of healing if they are to be successful in dealing with their problems and charting their own course. Parents are most useful when they act as a bridge or 'connectors' between the needs of adult children and service providers.

So, what is a parent to do...

For starters......

-Important to be available and listen to your adult children, they need to talk and vent as much as you do - better you than someone else who might also be in crisis.

-Allow and help your children find their own solutions before taking any action

-Better to nurture without necessarily rescuing but be on stand-by just in case

-Keep in mind that, ultimately, it is your adult children's responsibility for their crisis

---

Try to avoid...

... acting impulsively and without reflection can lead to inappropriate and guided intervention that can make matters worse for everyone

... rushing to the rescue. Helicopters should be grounded as it's far too tempting to quickly descend on n adult a child in distress whether you are wanted or even needed

...indecision and not investing time, energy and support when there is a real emergency could prove fatal and perpetuate a worsening situation

---

Finding Solutions.....

- *The more you listen to your adult children and give them an opportunity to vent, the more clues you will get with regards to how they perceive their problem and, more importantly, what kind of solutions they can bring to the table. Don't underestimate their own abilities to navigate their crises; sometimes all they need is a little empathy and support from you, not your excess worrying.*

- *At the same time, know when a critical situation is beyond what your family can handle – there is no shame in consulting others and getting professional help when the well being of your adult children is at risk.*

- *Step in when <u>necessary</u>, help out <u>within reason</u>, and step out while <u>empowering</u>.*

Check these references...

Publications on Adult Children in Crisis:

✓ What children can tell us about living in danger.
  J Garbarino, K Kostelny, N Dubrow - American
  Psychologist, 1991 - psycnet.apa.org

✓ Burdens and gratifications of caregiving: appraisal of
  parental care of adults with schizophrenia.
  MW Bulger, A Wandersman... - Am J Orthopsychiatry.
  1993 Apr;63(2):255-65 - psycnet.apa.org

On the Internet:

- When Crisis Hits | Focus on the Family
  www.focusonthefamily.com/parenting/parenting-
  challenges/...adult.../when-crisis-hits

- Establishing Boundaries With Adult Kids | Focus on the
  Family
  www.focusonthefamily.com/.../set...adult.../establishing-
  boundaries-with-adult-kids

- How can parents stop enabling and set boundaries for adult
  children? ... Enabling parents know that we live either
  smack dab in the middle of crisis or we' re ...

- Helping Adult Children Through Rough Times - Dr. Kathy
  McCoy ...
  drkathleenmccoy.blogspot.com/2012/06/helping-adult-
  children-through-rough.html

- What to do when your adult children are ruining your
  retirement - The ...
  www.theglobeandmail.com › Globe Investor › Retirement ›
  Family

- Six Ways to Help an Adult Child Face a Crisis - LifeWay
  www.lifeway.com/Article/mature-living-six-ways-to-help-an-
  adult-child-face-a-crisis

- When adult children fail, parents suffer too - CNN.com
  www.cnn.com/2010/HEALTH/08/12/adult.children.struggle/

- Prayer for Adult Children with Problems || Prayer Ideas
  www.prayerideas.org/wp/praying_for.../prayer-for-adult-
  children-with-problems/

When Adult Children Suffer from Mental Illness – Helpless and Frightened Parents

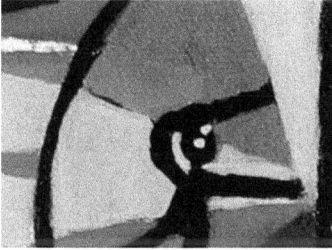

What the Freaken ...

Parents aren't always aware when their adult children are in the midst of an emotional crisis or, worse, when they are suffering from a serious mental health problem. They, also, rarely have any advance notice or clear indication that this calamity is about to hit their family. As can be expected, their response to this revelation is one of bewilderment followed by feelings of confusion and helplessness in not knowing what they should do next. For most, there follows a deep felt anxiety and worry and fear for the worse after hearing about their adult children's plight and afflictions.

Initial surprise and even disbelief ...

... "Oh my God, how could this have happened, things were going so well"

... "My son went crazy, out of control – what the hell happened?"

... **"When I was given the diagnosis, I felt that I'd been hit by a mac truck"**

Brings out shame, embarrassment, guilt and disappointment...

... **"I was ashamed of my son's near failure in his first semester of college (my alma mater) that I suffered all night in silence at a recent school reunion"**

... **"It probably runs in my family, but I didn't want to admit that it could strike us"**

... **"Where did I go wrong as a parent?"**

... **"They were headed towards rewarding careers when this happened – can they ever get back on track - was it all our fault that things went by the wayside"**

Leads to anxiety and worry...

..."**Now whenever the phone rings my adrenaline spikes and I break into a cold sweat"**

..."**We were recently informed that my son, just like my daughter, suffers from bipolar disorder - now both are out of school and going nowhere"**

... **"I get panic attacks at night just thinking what terrible things will happen to my daughter**

And fright and trepidation as to what to do and expect ...

… **"My son bites my head off if I should ever suggest that he needs some help to cope"**

… **"The probability of my having to support them is a frightening prospect, given my age and limited means"**

… **"I'm too old to care for my grandkids but who else is going to step in"**

… **"Will she ever get better, you know back to leading a normal life"**

What on earth is going on?

Various forms of mental illness afflict millions of adults and their families every year in North America. It is estimated that as many as one in five individuals suffer from some sort of anxiety disorder and depression and that more serious syndromes and anti-social behaviour can account for as much as 1% to 2% of the population. For those adults who suffer from a serious mental illness, it substantially interferes with or limits the involvement or participation in certain life activities (e.g. studies, jobs, social life). Furthermore, in both Canada and the U.S., it is estimated that over half of this population also experience a co-concurring substance use disorder.

In the emerging adult years, mental health issues related to anxiety, depression and phobias are so prevalent that, for the most part, they are considered as accompanying stress and almost inevitable baggage in the process of growing up. Where matters become more critical is when these young adults are diagnosed with more serious psychiatric disorders such as bi-polar disorder, schizophrenia and borderline personality and anti social disorders that appear to be on the rise. While young adults suffering from general depression and anxiety will have some motivation to seek help and eventually get better, those with more serious disorders are not cognisant or willing to engage in any treatment.

The stigma of mental illness is pervasive and impacts profoundly in how people deal with it, particularly when it hits home and directly affects loved ones. At the onset, there is a general tendency for both parents and adult children to be in denial of their situation and oblivious to the changes that are taking place around them. Invariably, the reality quickly sets in and parents have little choice but to react, albeit in ways that sometimes are not always constructive.

The natural response...

These situations and issues that present themselves are not within most parents' comfort zone or issues that they have any experience or facility in confronting. A common reaction by some parents, once again, is denial and wishful thinking that, maybe, there isn't a problem after all. Maybe it will pass and things will return to normal...

... **"Everyone gets depressed at one time or another, it'll pass like everything else he's gone through"**

... **"She keeps on telling us that she's very anxious these days – but you know she creates her own stress by always worrying about everything"**

... **"Once my daughter gets away from some of her bad friends and gets a job..."**

Some parents are uninformed as to what they are dealing with and misguided in their efforts to help....

... **"My child going on medication scares the hell out of me – you know the side effects and once you're on, you can't get off"**

... **"These things (schizophrenia) happen because of dysfunctional families and evil spirits – I pray everyday for God's help and trust in his guidance"**

... **"Maybe it's something I said or did that set him off... I was too hard and demanding... maybe I can make it up"**

And what do the professionals advise...

Many different conditions varying in severity of symptoms and level of dysfunction are frequently lumped together under the general diagnosis of mental illness. It is not uncommon for people to talk about anxiety, depression, phobia, and paranoia in the same breadth as bipolar, schizophrenia, borderline personality and psychotic behaviour. They are all, it is argued, conditions that essentially separated those that are 'normal' from those who are 'abnormal' or even crazy in their behaviour. The reality is that, diagnostically, each of these conditions is different and poses certain challenges in their treatment. As a general rule, those suffering from mental illness tend to have a distorted view of reality leading them to conclude that it is not themselves but others who have a problem. This is especially the case with the more serious diagnosis such as schizophrenia or borderline personality disorder where those suffering from these conditions cannot or will rarely if ever admit that they are the ones exhibiting problematic behaviour.

It is to be expected that parents are often completely in the dark as to what is going on in the minds of their children. Many young adults may break down only in their first few years of college or a new job that they fought so hard to get. In many cases, they fall prey to converging stressors that seem to come from all direction and make them far too vulnerable and emotionally unstable. Incipient mental illness can also be present and suddenly become symptomatic, often confusing and frightening these young adults as they struggle to maintain some sense of stability. Add to this boiling cauldron the fact that they are no longer minors and have every right to determine a treatment when and if they decide to act and you end up with parents who, with the best intentions, are over their heads in their effort to help their children.

What parents should know before doing anything

➢ As adult children go through a maturing process, there is a greater tendency for them to become more aware of their mental health condition and assume responsibility for doing something about it.

➢ Remember, adult children are just that, adults – treating them as little children, even if their behaviour warrants it, will only exacerbate matters and create more barriers to already strained relations.

➢ When parents allow themselves to assume blame and feel guilty for their adult children's mental health issues, they, inadvertently, set themselves up to be manipulated. The result is that these young adults never assume responsibility for their condition or treatment.

Being informed and having a good understanding of the situation

➢ Parents who suspect that their adult children have a mental health problem should become very familiar with their condition and the available resources that need to be mobilized.

➢ Before intervening with their adult children, parents should try to reflect and examine their own biases and prejudices as this will help them to be less judgemental and better able to empathize with their children.

Differentiating mental illness diagnosis

➢ Mental illness is not a one size fits all. On the contrary, there is a major difference between someone who suffers from a neurotic behavioural disorder and someone who is afflicted by clinical depression or anti social disorders and psychotic episodes.

➤ Informing oneself as to what exactly your adult children are experiencing and what drives their strange or unacceptable behaviour is a necessary and basic step to take before envisioning further intervention.

When children refuse or are not interested in getting help

➤ It is only when children grow up that parents become aware that there is something wrong in their behaviour and life situation. Unfortunately, by this time parents can expect a much more difficult and, sometime, impossible task of getting them to seek treatment.

➤ Parents who suspect that their adult children have a mental health problem should become very familiar with their condition and the available resources that need to be mobilized.

➤ If it is concluded that their condition does not pose a risk to their own well being or those of others in their care (for example, grandchildren), parents should remain on the sideline and be available when they are more ready to accept help. In more serious situations, however, more decisive actions might be warranted and should be taken.

➤ The challenge is for parents to get involved and be of assistance while being aware that some of their well-meaning actions can drive away and alienate the very persons they seek to help.

Parental intervention when dealing with less severe conditions

➤ It is incumbent on parents to avoid acting impulsively when finding out that their adult children are having mental health problems. Determining the nature of the problem and the degree of severity is important before intervening.

➤ If the actions of adult children do not pose serious danger to anyone including themselves, parents would do well to still maintain a strong presence and interest in their lives – that is, becoming informed (of condition and available resources) and encouraging their children to get help. Being overly forceful and imposing in these situations, will only drive the children away.

Parental intervention when dealing with more serious mental illness

➤ In those instances when a mental health condition (diagnosed or not) actually or potentially put the adult children or others in immediate or anticipated danger, it is incumbent on parents, as hard as it might be, to be proactive and not stand by passively waiting for something to happen.

➤ If this danger involves a suspected violent act or a suicidal attempt, parents need to alert police or any other professional or crisis center that might be able to effectively intervene. Issues of safety should not be compromised in order to 'protect' a loved one.

➢ As a last resort, parents should give serious consideration to taking legal action and have the courts force an adult child to undergo a psychiatric evaluation when the latter absolutely refuses to seek any help. Subject to an assessment and court order, these individuals suffering from serious mental illness (e.g. schizophrenia) and unwilling to collaborate in a prescribed treatment plan can be taken into care and, in some instances, obliged to take their medication.

Parental care

➢ When parents become frustrated and exhausted in their efforts to help their adult children cope, it is wise to simply step back and take the necessary time to re-assess and re-coup. There is no shame in taking a much-needed time out and re-charging the batteries on a personal and even financial level.

➢ It can be very useful and insightful for parents to join self-help groups set up for people like themselves who need support and information.

➢ Given the challenges and demands that face parents, it becomes important to work together and seek the support of other family members, community and professionals.

So, what is a parent to do...

For starters...

- Before you can be of help to your adult children, it becomes essential that you understand exactly what it is that they are experiencing and is dysfunctional for them.

- Obtaining information from various sources and especially from your children as to how they perceive their 'condition' can be an important step in eventually deciding what to do.

Try to avoid.........

... coming to the rescue simply because your adult children are displaying odd or disturbing behaviour

... prematurely diagnosing their behaviour or condition and prescribing treatment

---

Finding Solutions...

+ As hard as it might be for you not to overact and launch a rescue of your children, when they appear in distress, not rushing in to offer help will give you a more rational perspective as to what you can do.

+ Sit down with your children and relate to them that you are concerned about their well being and that you would like to offer your help and support.

+ Remember, you need not deal with these difficult situations alone and can share your concerns with other family members and professionals when necessary.

⊥ Check these references...

Publications on Adult Children and Mental Illness:

✓ Young, J. (2013). **When Your Adult Child Breaks Your Heart: Coping with Mental Illness, Substance Abuse, and the Problem that Tears Families Apart.** Conneticut:Guilfor Press.

✓ Being a parent of an adult son or daughter with severe mental illness receiving   professional care: parents' narratives
A Pejlert - Health & social care in the community,   2001 - Wiley Online Library

✓ Burdens and gratifications of caregiving: appraisal of parental care of adults with schizophrenia.
MW Bulger, A Wandersman... - American Journal of ..., 1993 - psycnet.apa.org

✓ The Long Term Impact of Parenting an Adult Child with Bipolar ...
https://books.google.ca/books?isbn=0549385274

✓ Positive parent/adult child relationships: impact of severe mental illness and caregiving burden. SA Pickett, JA Cook, BJ Cohler... - American Journal of ..., 1997 - psycnet.apa.org

On the Internet:

- Gaining Support When You Have a Troubled Adult Child | Psychology
...https://www.psychologytoday.com/.../gaining-support-when-you-have-troubled-adult..

  - Setting Boundaries with a Mentally Ill Adult Child - Focus

on the Family
family.custhelp.com/app/.../a_id/.../setting-boundaries-with-
a-mentally-ill-adult-   child

-   High Stress Levels in Parents of Adult Children with Mental
    Illness www.goodtherapy.org/blog/stress-parents-children-
    mental-illness-0213123/

- A parent's fight: Caring for an adult child with mental
  illness | News OK newsok.com/article/3843285

- What We Didn't Say: A struggle — parenting children with
  mental illness www.cmhnetwork.org/media...zen/a-struggle-
  parenting-children-with-mental-illness

Problems of Substance Abuse, Incarceration and Self Destructive Practices – A nightmare for Parents

What the Freaken ....

Parents are often shocked when they are faced with their adult children's substance abuse problem, incarceration or life threatening situation that suddenly takes over family functioning like a bad dream from which they can't seem to wake up. If only they would have seen it coming or had prepared for such bad new. Reactions include:

Initial surprise and even disbelief …

… "It's a 'freaken' shame, as usual, bad things always seem to happen to good people"

… "Oh my good God! Now what the hell do we do, who do we call?"

… "It can't be Alan, why he's never even smoked a joint, I know that for a fact!"

Brings out shame, embarrassment, guilt and disappointment…

… "I always told her she was in an abusive relationship, she wouldn't listen and now this!"

… **"Four generations of Masons and never a problem, now we have to face this mess"**

… **"I didn't come to this country to have my son end up in jail for some crazy thing.."**

Leads to anxiety and worry…

…**"If she stays on the street, I'm afraid she'll die for sure…how can I get to her before things get worse?"**

…**"I can't bear to think what will happen to him now that he's inside"**

… **"I'm so petrified that my only child will end up finding a way to end her life"**

And fright and trepidation as to what to do and expect …

… **"Please don't tell me they put him in that hell hole with serious criminals"**

… **"Please, there must be someone, some place that can help my son, there can't be nothing available, for God's sake!"**

What on earth is going on?

Without any doubt, whenever you have adult children that find themselves dependent on drugs or alcohol, are incarcerated for various criminal acts or become mired with self destructive thoughts and actions, you also, more than likely, have distraught and stressed out parents struggling to make sense of these events and trying to desperately figure out what they need to do. Substance abuse and incarceration among young adults in both the U.S. and Canada has reached epidemic levels that pose a serious threat to family functioning and social stability. The use of illegal drugs of all types and the abuse of alcohol and prescription medication is widespread and while it affects all socioeconomic groups, it is particularly rampant among 20 to 35 year old men and women. Most tragically, the number of young people who commit suicide or have suicidal ideation has equally reached alarming proportions and is one of the leading causes of death in North America. Not surprisingly, researchers have found positive correlations between substance abuse, incarceration and suicide for this target population. No wonder, most parents over react with emotions when confronted with these nightmarish events.

The natural response…

Although it can be argued that a parent is not legally responsible for their adult children's bad choices in life, most continue to feel responsibility for their transgressions and the burden of setting everything right. Ironically, these personal and family crises, while having a tendency to undermine all the past 'good' parenting practices, have a tendency to bring out the most visceral parental reaction. Some get into an automatic rescue mode where there is little thought to how much energy and financial should be expended while other parents might initially react with angry indignation that their own flesh and blood could do such a terrible thing. Across the board, however, it is heated emotions and embarrassment or shame that usually exacerbate an already volatile situation. These mixed but strong reactions can include rationalizing an unacceptable behaviour, blaming other persons or influences and just simply walking away from the problem altogether….

… **"When you are desperate, you know, you'll do anything to survive"**

… **"She was duped in doing it by her crazy friends, she would have never done it on her own"**

… **"He's not a little kid anymore, he made his bed, he'll unfortunately have to lie in it"**

A majority of parents, while hurt and angry, are consumed by shame, regret of not having done more, and a heavy heart that keep them at their children's beck and call….

… **"I wasn't around when it counted, I can at least try to make it up now"**

…**"It's a terrible mistake that he now seems to regret, better later than never "**

… **"You know, it breaks my heart to see her in such a desperate state and always in tears "**

... **"Money is no obstacle, I'll do whatever it will take to get him out of this mess and functioning again "**

Finally, some parents look elsewhere for guidance and even deliverance....

... **"I'll put my trust in God, surely he is in the know as to what we should do"**

... **"Don't worry, I'm owed and this guy, believe you me, will take care of everything"**

... **" I'm am confident that justice will prevail"**

And what do the professionals advise...

To be sure, there is no shortage of expert advice on such a hot topic that affects nearly one in ten people in our country, and that's on a good day. Everywhere you turn, it seems, there are surveys, research studies, articles, books and countless blogs on the subject as well as a plethora of mushrooming services that purportedly claim to 'cure' anyone with the means to afford treatment. In the U.S. and Canada, there are literally thousands of substance abuse treatment programs that provide residential, hospitalization and out patient services along with a prodigious number of therapists and counsellors offering short and long term interventions and using a smorgasbord of approaches and techniques. And, of course, let's not forget all of those lawyers that are more than eager to represent and fight for those who find themselves caught in the criminal justice system. Business is definitely good but are the results worthy of the hype. As in all human endeavours, there is the positive side to all this and the less savoury aspect, that is, unscrupulous vendors of services preying on the unsuspecting and those most vulnerable for instant results.

Adult children are frequently tempted with the need to self medicate in order to deal with their life problems and parents are, subsequently, faced with the impossible task of wading through a jungle trying to pick up the pieces and get their children on the right path. So, what is a distraught, emotionally vulnerable and frustrated parent to do and how do they expend the limited energy and financial resources available to them? Most parents have a great deal of difficulty trying to take the first few steps and being able to separate the wheat from the shaft when it comes to professional help and community services. The following doesn't purport to offer quick fix prescriptions for very complex issues that impact differentially on each troubled and misguided young adult. Nevertheless, there is good available information, suggestions and even possible solutions that are important for parents and other family members to consider as they struggle with what often seems for them to be a perpetual nightmare.

What parents should know before doing anything

➢ Putting things in perspective can be helpful in getting a better understanding of what just happened or has been happening to your adult children. In the first place, keep in mind whose problem this is and who created the mess in the first place. Adult children generally possess the ability to discern right from wrong and should always be held accountable for their transgressions. This will allow them to hopefully heal and move on.

➢ It is not unusual for parents to drift towards self-blame and guilt - remember that you, as a parent are not perfect beings and more than likely did the best you could under the circumstances. Besides, however remiss you might feel, the past is behind you and it is the present and future that need attention. Ruminating about what should have been can contribute greatly to inaction and commiseration.

➢ There is a distinction between loving and caring for your adult children and 'enabling' them. The <u>less you 'rescue' and the more you 'empower them'</u> to take responsibility for their actions, the more they will become safe and self sufficient.

➢ While your adult children might need your attention, don't forget that your other family members are also in need of attention and sheltered from the fall out of this protracted battle with substance abuse and repeated run-ins with the law. Provide other family members with appropriate explanations and even literature on the problem being experienced so as to have everyone, especially the other parent, on the same page.

➢ Addiction is more of a disease and subject to personal life choices than a moral issue or reflective of the quality of the person suffering from it.

Being informed and having a good understanding of the situation

➢ Having a clear understanding of what exactly is going on and what are the implications for the adult children and family are important pieces of information that can make a real difference in how a parent might respond. All too often, there is a tendency to get into a panic mode that, invariably, creates excessive and misguided rescue missions or non-involvement. Relapse is also quite common and should be anticipated and factored into whatever plan of intervention is being devised.

➢ Substance abuse among young people is not a simple phenomenon and neither is it a single isolated event in their lives. More often than not it is an on-going problem that is linked to past experiences and present circumstances (personal, social, financial and work related) that might challenge their resolve and ability to cope. Added to this is the fact that these problems will often incite young people to commit crimes to sustain their habits and even contemplate suicide when matters look ominous and hopeless. The better a parent understands the whole picture, the more effective and successful the intervention.

➤ Some type of professional intervention is usually warranted and necessary.

When children refuse or are not interested in getting help

➤ It is not uncommon for adult children hooked on drugs and alcohol to be oblivious to the fact that they have a serious problem requiring some sort of intervention. In these instances, a parent needs to consult a trained professional in the field and get some insight and direction as to how to proceed. This is especially critical when you have depressed young adults threatening to end their lives as discouragement turns into despondence and hopelessness. Most often, parents don't have a clue as to what is going on and even less power to intervene.

➤ When adult children are putting themselves in danger or are being self destructive or a threat to others and refuse help, parents don't have any choice but to signal them to the appropriate authorities and allow them to step in and, hopefully, take charge. The old saying "better alive than dead" is never more pertinent.

➤ If they refuse to collaborate but there is no imminent danger of harm parents are well advised to back off temporarily but to keep a watchful eye as to when it might be more opportune to intervene. Telling troubled but uncooperative adult children that they are always loved and that the door is always open should they be ready to get help can be an important life-line that parents can extend.

Parental intervention when dealing with substance abuse

➢ There is a great deal of research and general information on substance abuse with regards to young adults. Parents should take the opportunity to peruse the literature and become well acquainted with what it is, what gives rise to it and what treatments work best.

➢ To be effective in dealing with this issue, parents need to take a non-judgemental but caring and concerned stance when interacting with their adult children. Stepping back and letting the emotions calm down will help in allowing parents to listen more and condemn less, a great formula for moving forward. Also, managing one's expectations is critical as recovery takes time and usually involves many potential setbacks before success is attained.

➢ Parents, in being enabling, can ask their adult children suffering addiction to explore what they would envision as being different or changing should, by miracle, things improve in their lives. Also, having them reflect on what kind of personal and family narrative they would like to construct for themselves and for their own progeny can kick start a process of findings solutions and re-scripting one's life.

Parental intervention when dealing with suicidal ideation and threats

➢ When adult children announce to their parents that they have intentions of killing themselves, they are either reacting to feelings of depression and despondence or they use the manoeuvre to extract money from their parents usually used to feed an addiction. In either case, parents become highly stressed and anxious about the possibility of losing their child and feel trapped in a no win situation.

➢ If a parent becomes aware that their adult son or daughter is having suicidal ideations or expresses intentions of actually committing suicide and they don't want to do anything about it, it is incumbent on the parents to call 911 or any other local emergency organization that can respond with immediacy and professional competence. It is an emergency needing immediate attention.

➢ Suicidal ideations and gestures can be repeated over a long period of time unless the root causes are dealt with in therapy. As such, parents are encouraged to become connected to suicide hot lines and self help groups where they can share their predicament with other parents.

Parental care

➤ Parents are of not much use in helping their children deal with problems of dependency, incarceration or despondency if they are unable to take care of themselves with regards to their own mental and physical health and make judicious use of their limited financial resources in providing support. As in many other crisis situations, parents should be mindful of their own limits and well being.

➤ Organizations like Al-Anon, Nar-Anon and Parents of Suicide offer parent support programs that are generally very helpful to those parents whose children are suffering addiction or are suicidal. Sharing with other parents in similar situations can be very relieving and empowering.

➤ Save some energy and even put aside some money for yourself as you'll need some respite as you embark on what might be a very long journey towards recovery. For most recovering addicts, it is a life-time commitment to stay sober and clean and this, invariably, implicates all those around them.

So, what is a parent to do...

<u>For starters</u>.....

- As a parent, you need to constantly remind yourself of the fact that your children are now adults and have, essentially, the ability to distinguish right from wrong and what it is that puts them at risk.
- Tell yourself that it is not, really, your problem but one that they need to own and for which they need to be accountable. This way it is not expected that you will provide all the solutions and the resources needed to fix it.
- Listen, first and foremost, to what your children have to say about their predicament before gathering more information from other sources and deciding what to do (if anything).

<u>Try to avoid</u>......

... treating your children as misfits or derelicts that have bad judgement

... being overly critical and judgemental as your adult children also have feelings and don't like being reprimanded – telling them 'I told you so' is a sure way of losing them

... being a 'hawk-eyed' parent who will pluck your adult children out of any danger in which they find themselves – it doesn't work and they don't develop 'good judgement'

Finding Solutions.....

- Once you, as a parent, have made an effort to separate your own ideas, values and preferences from those of your adult children, it certainly becomes a little easier to be objective in assessing their predicament and how you need to intervene, if at all.
- The best solutions are, obviously, those that are arrived at by the very same persons that created the problem. As such, it is a wise parent who will step back and help their adult children to figure out their own path to recovery and well being.
- To be sure, when they are at risk or in danger, there is a need for direct intervention, preferably well armed and with a supporting cast.

Check these references...

Publications on Dealing with Adult Children with Problems of Substance Abuse, Incarceration and Self Destructive Practices:

✓ **Verbal and physical abuse as stressors in the lives of lesbian, gay male, and bisexual   youths: associations with school problems, running away, substance abuse.** RC Savin-Williams - Journal of consulting and clinical psychology, 1994 - psycnet.apa.org

✓ **Outcome, attrition, and family–couples treatment for drug abuse: A meta-analysis and review of the controlled, comparative studies.**
MD Stanton, WR Shadish - Psychological bulletin, 1997 - psycnet.apa.org

✓ **Cycles of pain: Risk factors in the lives of incarcerated mothers and their children**
S Greene, C Haney, A Hurtado - The Prison Journal, 2000 - tpj.sagepub.com

✓ **Family factors in youth suicidal behaviors**
BM Wagner, MAC Silverman... - American Behavioral ..., 2003 - abs.sagepub.com

On the Internet:

- **Developmental trauma disorder - The Trauma Center**

   www.traumacenter.org/products/pdf_files/preprint_dev_trau ma_disorder.pdf

- **Freeing the Parents of Adult Alcoholics and Addicts -**

GoodTherapy.org
www.goodtherapy.org/blog/freeing-the-parents-of-adult-
alcoholics-and-addicts/

- Substance Abuse Problems
  Adwww.centeronaddiction.org/

- How to Let Go of Codependency and Take Care of Yourself
  cathytaughinbaugh.com/are-you-ready-to-let-go-of-
  codependency-and-take-care-of-..

- Parent of drug addict help: Top 10 truths to help parents |
  Addiction Blog
  drug.addictionblog.org/parent-of-drug-addict-help-top-10-
  truths-to-help-parents/

- Detaching With Love: How I Learned to Separate My Son and
  His ...
  www.drugfree.org/detaching-with-love-how-i-learned-to-
  separate-my-son-and-his-ad.

Relationships and Lifestyle Choices – Unsettling Revelations for Parents

What the Freaken ....

It's quite shocking and unsettling, to say the least, when parents are unexpectedly confronted by their 'grown up' children with a new spin on life and set of priorities that sometimes make little sense to them. The reactions vary and it takes these parents time to fully recover from the onslaught and make sense of it all.

Initial surprise and even disbelief ...

> ... **"I was so shocked when I received harsh criticism from my son... he used to be so gentle he would have never said boo to a goose"**

> ... **"You've changed so much, I hardly recognize who you are anymore"**

> ... **"The real you is a what? I never saw this coming, you got to be kidding me"**

Brings out anger and disappointment...

> ..."**It hurts me to say it but my daughter turns into an idiot when it comes to sizing up guys and their real intentions**"

… "We sacrificed a lot to get her through college…and all of that for what, a moron who doesn't even have a job"

… "I saw her coming from a mile away, and Joe suddenly can't seem to see past his nose"

… "She moves in with you, I'm no longer going to subsidize the rent…I'm sorry bu this is more than I can handle…you'll always be my daughter but I feel so betrayed!"

Leads to anxiety and worry…

…"O.K, so I'll shut up…but that woman is going to drag him into the poor   house…and then what?"

…"Oh my God, I can't believe my daughter allows herself to be treated this way…this is not going to get better"

… "My grandkids should not be dragged into this, this is between me and my son and and has nothing to do with them, not even his wife"

… "So much for grandchildren, I guess"

What on earth is going on?

While children are young, parents have almost full control and the last say over everything they do. As they became older, this control shifts to them and parents are faced with the discomfort of slowly taking a back seat in the family car. Normally, this can be a relatively smooth transition that tends to accelerate after the minor children become adults and are 'launched' into the world to deal with their own separate lives. Marriage leads to grandchildren and the cycle completes itself. With some parents, however, this life cycle doesn't turn the corner so smoothly. For many, this change-over in autonomy is greatly delayed and unanticipated circumstances lead to strained relations and resentment.

Much of the research on parent-adult children relations indicates that it is not a breakdown in communication and interactional styles that are most problematic but rather differences in the values held and personal habits and lifestyle choices made by the adult children. These disagreements, unfortunately, tend to escalate quickly and end up in the proverbial 'red zone' where serious damage can occur to the newly minted 'adult to adult' relationships. Adult children most often create their own value system with respect to personal relationships, marriage, child rearing, religion, work orientation household maintenance and even politics. Their lifestyle choices in terms of whom they choose as partners, how and where and they end up living and even sexual orientation which as strange as it my appear to parents, can actually change inadvertently as witnessed by the emergence of transgender and transsexual people who can have any sexual orientation.

The natural response...

Unlike many other responses that come natural to parents, differences in values and lifestyle choices seem to elicit reactions that reflect strongly held belief systems and deeply rooted sense of what is good and what is not. Even parents who see themselves as 'progressive boomers' and 'au current' are inclined to feel unsure and uncomfortable about some of the things their progeny do and say. Some of these revelations are such an obstacle for them to get around that parents, as we have previously mentioned, will initially revert to denial and wishful thinking that maybe there isn't a problem after all and maybe it will pass and things will return to normal.

... **"This will pass like everything else he's done and said...let's give it time"**

... **"You know, when children come into the picture, they'll have to mature up"**

... **"They weren't brought up by wolves, sooner or later what we taught them and who they really are is going to kick in"**

Some parents are uninformed as to what they are dealing with and misguided in their efforts to help....

... **"When I sit down with this guy and read the riot act, believe you me things are going to change"**

... **"She definitely needs some help here...and I know just the person who can set her straight on this "**

Resignation of the inevitable…

> … **"In our day, I guess we were a little wild, but this is crazy and I have no idea where this is going"**

> … **"I'm just saying, sometimes the police can't do anything and the legal system, well, forget it"**

And what do the professionals advise…..

Unquestionably, what is most difficult for the majority of parents is to restrain themselves from giving an unsolicited opinion or advice to their adult children when it seems obvious to them that relationships and lifestyle choices appear to be misguided. During the formative years leading to adulthood, parents, with all good intentions, tend to be very involved in shaping their children's thoughts and actions. Problems usually arise when their children reach age of majority and the time comes for them to be ready for a successful launch as independent individuals. The process of individuation that should normally take place during this period of time is often thwarted in favour of continuing to maintain some measure of control on the part of parents.

Other than in exceptional cases, parents generally mean well and truly want to be helpful, protective and keep their grown up children on a 'good' path. After all, they are still parents and they have invested so much throughout the years. Yet, parents do need to seriously reflect on what it is that they are standing ground on and whose interests they are really defending. The family narrative is changing and so are the actors who write the script.

When values and lifestyle choices clash

➢ Adult children have a right to their own set of values and priorities in life. When these clash with those held by parents, any effort to steer them in the right direction might be met with resentment and lead to distance and even estrangement.

➢ As a general rule, when adult children make lifestyle decisions, parental opinion and advice should be kept to a minimum unless such personal choices will create serious consequences and regrets.

Choice of partners and new relationships

➢ Being critical of a son's or daughter's romantic interest can land parents in the proverbial 'dog house' or worse come back to haunt the future 'parent in law'. As such it's probably wise and the right thing to do if parents kept their opinion to themselves and act cordially towards any of their adult children's love interests. After all it is their life and their choice.

➢ Parents need to make every effort to get along with their adult children's husbands and wives as, in the end, toxic relations can adversely affect the quality and frequency of contact with their own children and grandchildren. It becomes a sad day when adult children severe contact with their parents or when grandparents have to turn to the courts to facilitate visits.

When should a parent intervene

➢ Most experts who weigh in on the subject are of the opinion that parents have a right if not an obligation to intervene when they conclude that their adult children are being victimized by their significant others. There should be no tolerance for abusive behaviour and any action (legal and non criminal of course) taken by a parent is not considered as interfering in the their lives but as being protective of their well being.

Parental care

➢ If irreconcilable differences impede a respectful and meaningful relationship with their adult children, parents need to address their own difficulty in letting go of their control and expectations and begin to accept their 'not so little children' for who they are. Getting help from friends, religious leaders and professionals is not only advisable but commendable.

So, what is a parent to do...

For starters...

- Make every effort to understand why you are reacting so strongly to your adult children's values and lifestyle choices

- Be objective and try to assess whether what they think and do is truly problematic and risky behaviour that might put someone in danger or are they simply strange and, perhaps, unwholesome lifestyle choices

- Be as respectful, accepting and tolerant as possible and express opinion and give advice exceptionally and only when solicited

---

Try to avoid...

... quick and spontaneous reactions that are usually taken without reflection

... being judgemental and critical of your adult children's values and lifestyle choices

... interfering with the way your adult children choose to live their lives

---

Finding Solutions.....

+ If values and lifestyle choices made by adult children are not contested or considered by parents to be either threatening or unacceptable, there is a greater possibility for dialogue and understanding leading to a more respectful adult to adult relationship.

+ When communication and dialogue are facilitated and based on mutual respect, it becomes easier to deal with problematic situations and accept compromise and change,

+ As adult children are given greater opportunities to define their own path in life, they generally develop, over time, a capacity to generate their proper solutions when problems arise.

⚓ Check these references...

Publications on Relationships and Lifestyle Choices:

✓ Bridging the Gap Between Adult Children and ... - ScholarlyCommons
repository.upenn.edu/cgi/viewcontent.cgi?article=1043&context=edissertations...

✓ Types of Conflicts and Tensions Between Older Parents and Adult ...
gerontologist.oxfordjournals.org/content/39/3/261.short?rss=1&ssource=mfr

✓ Reciprocity in parent–child relations over the adult life course
M Silverstein, SJ Conroy... - The Journals ..., 2002
psychsocgero
ntology.oxfordjournals.

✓ The role of parents in the socialization of children: An historical overview.
EE Maccoby - Developmental psychology, 1992 -
psycnet.apa.org

On the Internet:

- Parenting Adult Children Who Make Bad Choices - Kevin A. Thompson
www.kevinathompson.com/how-to-parent-an-adult-child-who-is-making-bad-decision.

- How to Handle Feeling Disappointment with Your Adult Child
www.empoweringparents.com › Adult Children

- **Parental Influence: Telling Adult Children What to Do - GoodTherapy.org**
  www.goodtherapy.org/.../parental-influence-telling-adult-children-what-to-do-10201.

- **Parenting Our Adult Children - OnlineMinistries**
  onlineministries.creighton.edu/CollaborativeMinistry/.../ParentingAdultChildren.html

- **Lifestyle choices of adult children - Parenting tips- Parent Exchange**
  www.kidspot.com.au › Parenting › Family life

- **Types of Conflicts and Tensions Between Older Parents and Adult ...**
  gerontologist.oxfordjournals.org/content/39/3/261.full.pdf

<u>Needs of Parents of Adult Children</u>

The preceding texts have highlighted some of the most common situations and issues faced by parents of adult children. For most, family life and relationships do not always move along a smooth path or one of least resistance. That is why our 'beloved children' are sometimes, understandably, referred to as our 'freaken kids' who can, by their behavior or inaction, raise the level of anxiety and frustration beyond what is often tolerable and even acceptable. Nevertheless, it should be stressed that parents must be vigilant with regards to what is imposed on them and the manner in which they respond.

Parents have needs too and the right to enjoy the rest of their lives free of abuse, unreasonable demands made on their time and resources and to be able to live out their retirement in peace and tranquility. The following is a but a brief checklist of some of the most important things that you, as a parent, need to consider:

- ✓ As a parent, you are, after all, human and subject to making mistakes and can't be expected to always have all the answers to every problem faced by your adult children.

- ✓ Parents, like yourself, will always tend to worry and be pre-occupied about the well being of their adult children and grandchildren, especially when their lives take a turn for the worse. Nevertheless, you also have to focus on your own needs and what enhances your own well being. It's important to take the time and resources to do all the things that you are finally in a position to enjoy.

✓ Parents should not be obliged to loose personal integrity and the ability to make decision for themselves as they get older. You should spell out clearly and in advance as to what it is you expect your children to do in the event that you become incapable of doing things for yourself.

✓ As parents grow older, they are more easily imposed on and often manipulated into agreeing to every request made of them. Remember, you most certainly have a right to refuse to comply to any behavior and request that you feel is inappropriate and abusive of you as a parent and person.

✓ Most parents who prepare for retirement should be able to do just that, enjoy the 'golden years' without having to worry about debt and financial obligations to others. You owe yourself to finally relax and not 'have to go the office' because of extra needs presented by your adult children.

www.ingramcontent.com/pod-product-compliance
Lightning Source LLC
Chambersburg PA
CBHW071006040426
42443CB00007B/692